A Kitchen Love Story

Sue Leather and Julian Thomlinson

Series Editor: Rob Waring
Story Editor: Julian Thomlinson
Series Development Editor: Sue Leather

HEINLE
CENGAGE Learning™

Australia • Brazil • Japan • Korea • Mexico • Singapore • Spain • United Kingdom • United States

HEINLE
CENGAGE Learning

Page Turners Reading Library

A Kitchen Love Story
Sue Leather and Julian Thomlinson

Publisher: Andrew Robinson

Executive Editor: Sean Bermingham

Senior Development Editor:
Derek Mackrell

Assistant Editor: Sarah Tan

Director of Global Marketing:
Ian Martin

Content Project Manager:
Tan Jin Hock

Print Buyer:
Susan Spencer

Layout Design and Illustrations:
Redbean Design Pte Ltd

Cover Illustration: Eric Foenander

Photo Credits:
40 Michaeljung/Shutterstock
41 Dave Pullig/Flickr
42 Ariadna De Raadt/Shutterstock
43 (top to bottom)
Pennyimages/Shutterstock,
Richard Peterson/Shutterstock,
tezzstock/Shutterstock

ISBN-13: 978-1-4240-4639-3

ISBN-10: 1-4240-4639-4

Heinle
20 Channel Center Street
Boston, Massachusetts 02210
USA

Cengage Learning is a leading provider of customized learning solutions with office locations around the globe, including Singapore, the United Kingdom, Australia, Mexico, Brazil, and Japan. Locate your local office at:
international.cengage.com/region

Cengage Learning products are represented in Canada by Nelson Education, Ltd.

Visit Heinle online at **elt.heinle.com**

Visit our corporate website at
www.cengage.com

Printed in the United States of America
3 4 5 6 7 21 20 19 18 17

Contents

Background Reading

People in the story

Janine Cole
Janine works in the Brenton
College cafeteria. She has
a young daughter.

Amber Cole
Amber is Janine's
three-year-old daughter.

Randy Gordon
Randy studies communications
at Brenton College. He's also
a football player.

Hilary Johnson
Hilary is Randy's
ex-girlfriend. She is also a
communications student.

Gayle King
Gayle is manager of the college
cafeteria and Janine's boss.

Georges Ducasse
Georges is the head chef of
The Blue House restaurant
in Seattle.

This story is set in Brenton, a college town in the
northwestern United States.

Chapter 1

A kind act

"More cups, Janine!" shouted Gayle King.

Not again, thought Janine Cole. It was near the end of a busy lunchtime in the college cafeteria, and Janine felt tired. Janine's manager, Gayle, made her tired—she was always shouting.

Janine walked to the table near the window. As she walked across the room she looked at the clock on the wall. Two-thirty. It was almost time to pick up Amber, her little three-year-old daughter, from the babysitter's house. It cost money, but it was the only way that Janine could work. She walked more quickly.

She got to the table and started to put the dirty cups and plates onto her tray. *So many plates*, she thought. *Why couldn't the students put their things away?* There was food on the blue table-top. *I'm here to clean up after them*, she thought, *so they don't care. They don't know how lucky they are.* She cleaned the table and picked up the tray. It was heavy, but she started to walk back to the kitchen. Suddenly, she felt someone run into her. Her tray of cups and plates fell to the floor with a loud crash! Everyone in the room looked up.

"Hey!" Janine shouted.

It was a big, tall young man with blond hair.

"Sorry," he said.

"Sorry? What're you doing running around in here? This is a cafeteria, not a football field!" Janine was shouting, and her face was red. Everyone was looking at her, but she couldn't stop herself. "You think you can just run around everywhere, and other people have to clean up after you?"

"I'm really sorry," the young man said quietly. He started to pick things up and put them on the tray.

Gayle arrived. "I'm sorry about this," she said to the young man. "Please don't do that. We can do it."

Janine looked at the young man cleaning the mess up. She wanted to cry. But she didn't cry. She started to help him.

"Really, it's no problem," the young man said. "I did it, anyway."

"Joe, clean this up," Gayle called to one of the kitchen workers. Then, quietly, she said to Janine, "In my office. Now."

◇◇◇

"You shouted at that student," said Gayle. She was sitting behind her desk in her office. Janine was sitting in front of her.

"I know."

"You can't do that, Janine. You can't just shout at customers that way." Gayle looked into Janine's eyes. "I'm afraid you can't work here anymore. Please get your things and go . . ."

"Gayle, you know I really need this job."

"I know, Janine, but this isn't the first time, is it? You're always having problems with the students. Why, Janine? You were a student yourself, weren't you?"

It was true. Two years ago, Janine was training to be a chef. But then her husband, Chris, died. After that, Janine started working to support herself and her little girl, so she couldn't continue at college.

There was a knock on the door.

"I'm in a meeting!" Gayle called, but the door opened anyway. Janine turned around. It was the young man who ran into her. *What did he want?*

"I'm very sorry, ma'am," said the young man. "But I want to say something."

"What is it?" Gayle asked.

"My name's Randy Gordon, and I just want to say that she was right. I was running and I hit her. I wasn't looking where I was going. I mean, really. Ms. . . . um . . . She . . . ah . . ."

"Her name's Janine," Gayle said.

"Ms. Janine, well, she was right to shout at me. It was me."

Randy was a little red in the face.

"Anyway, I'll go now. Thank you," he said and left, closing the door.

Gayle turned back to Janine.

"That was nice of him, wasn't it?" Gayle said.

"Yes, it was," Janine replied quietly.

"Well, I'm really not sure . . ." Gayle said.

"Please, Gayle," said Janine quietly. She didn't like to ask, but she had to do it.

"You've got one more chance," Gayle said. "Don't do it again."

Chapter 2

Janine's dream

A few days later, Janine was shopping downtown with Amber when she saw Randy across the street. She began to cross.

"Where are we going, Mommy?" Amber said.

"We're going to talk to that young man."

"After that, can I have an ice cream?"

"After we talk to him, we'll go to the bank," said Janine. "If you sit quietly in the bank, I'll get you an ice cream."

"OK!" said the little girl, smiling.

She's such a good girl, Janine thought. *The one thing in my life that's good right now.*

"Um, excuse me," Janine said to Randy.

"Hey! It's you! Hi. How are you doing?" Randy smiled and looked at Amber. "Hey there!" he said. "What's your name, little girl?"

"Amber," she said, smiling back.

"I wanted to say thank you for the other day," Janine began. "And sorry for shouting at you. I was wrong."

"Hey, I was stupid, like you said."

"I didn't mean that," said Janine. "Anyway, thanks for speaking to Gayle. My manager. She can be . . . difficult."

"Hey, I can see that. It's no problem." Randy looked at her shopping bags. "Can I help with those?"

"No, it's fine," Janine said. "They're not heavy."

"Here," Randy said, taking one of the bags. "Where are we going?"

"Thanks. Just down to the bank," Janine replied. They started to walk. Randy was looking in the shopping bag.

"Chicken!" he said. "You like chicken, Amber?"

"I love Mommy's chicken," she said.

"I'm sure you do," Randy said.

"I love all Mommy's food," Amber went on. "Do you like Mommy's food?"

Janine's face went red. Randy laughed.

"Well, I didn't try it, Amber," he said to the child.

"Oh," Amber said.

Suddenly, Janine said, "You know, you could come for dinner one night? To say thank you, I mean."

"Great! I'd love to," Randy replied.

"I mean if you're not busy running into things all the time . . ."

They both laughed.

"I said I'd love to."

◇◇◇

"This is great!" Randy said.

"It's OK," replied Janine. "I mean, it's nothing special."

Janine, Randy, and Amber were in Janine's house, eating at the kitchen table.

"No, no, no. I'm telling you. This is really, really good. This is the best chicken I've ever had. I'm serious. What do you think, Amber?"

"Too much salt."

Randy laughed. "Too much salt, you say? Well, how about that?"

"She helps me in the kitchen a lot," Janine said. "And she learns things, you know."

They ate quietly for a while. Janine was thinking about the bank. After she saw Randy in the street, she went to the bank to ask for more money. She didn't have the money to pay the rent this month. But the bank said no.

"Hey, is everything all right?" Randy asked.

"I'm fine, I'm fine," Janine said.

After the chicken, they ate apple pie. Then Janine put Amber to bed. When she came back to the kitchen, Randy was washing the dishes.

"You don't need to do that," she said.

"It's OK. I'm almost finished," said Randy.

"How about some coffee? There's more apple pie, too."

"Yes, please!"

Janine made coffee, and they sat back down at the table.

"Tell me about you, then," Janine said. "All I know is that you're called Randy."

"Nothing much to say, really," he said. "I study communications. When I finish at Brenton, my father wants me to work with him. Oh, and I play football."

"I knew you played football or something," she said.

"You mean I look like a football player?" he smiled.

She looked at him. He was tall and had big, broad shoulders.

"You really look like a football player," she said, laughing.

"I guess I do," he said. "OK, so what about you? I know you work in the cafeteria . . . and I know you have a beautiful little daughter."

"Thank you," said Janine.

"And her father?"

"My husband, Chris . . . He died in a car crash two years ago," she said.

"Oh, Janine, I'm so sorry," Randy said. "Really, I didn't know . . ."

"It's OK. Of course you didn't."

They sat quietly for a moment.

"This apple pie is great, too, you know. Really wonderful," he said. "Better than the food in the cafeteria. Oh, I mean . . ."

"Ha!" she said. "Well, I only get to cook burgers and fries in the cafeteria . . ."

"Janine, with cooking like this, you could be a real chef. I mean, at a good restaurant."

"That's my dream. Or it was, anyway. I was studying to be a chef. But then Chris died, and . . . well . . ." She looked toward Amber's room.

"I see," said Randy. "I'm sorry. It must be difficult to bring up a child on your own."

"It is difficult sometimes," she said. Then she smiled. "But she's so lovely. I'm lucky, really. To have her, I mean."

"You really are," Randy agreed. Then suddenly he sat up, like he had an idea.

"Hey, listen. I just thought of something," he said. "One of my friends. She's studying to be a chef. She told me about this cooking competition. Do you know The Blue House in Seattle?"

"Of course," said Janine. The Blue House was one of the best restaurants in Seattle, maybe even in all of the U.S.

"My friend was telling me that they are having a cooking competition to find a new chef. The first prize in the competition is a job there, as a trainee chef."

A chef at The Blue House, Janine thought. *Wow . . .*

"Why don't you try the competition?" Randy said.

"Me?" Janine laughed. "No . . . I can cook a little, but The Blue House? Come on!"

"I'm serious, Janine. You know, I used to go to a lot of good restaurants with my family, and I'm telling you, that chicken, it's the best. Why don't you think about it?"

"I don't know, Randy. I don't think I can win a competition like that," Janine said.

"Well, you can't win if you don't enter it," he replied.

Chapter 3

Chicken Janine

A few days later, Janine called Randy.

"I'll do it," she said.

"Great!" he replied. "Can I meet you after lunch? I'll get the information for you."

"I finish at 2:45," she said. "Can you come before then?"

"Yeah, sure," he said.

Randy came to the cafeteria at 2:40. His face was very red. Janine came out of the kitchen to talk to him.

"Hey, are you all right?" she asked.

"Janine, the competition—it closes today!"

"What?! Are you serious?"

"I'm really sorry. I didn't know. You have to send them this form from their website." He was holding a piece of paper in his hand. "We can write it now and I can drive it up to Seattle this afternoon for you."

"Really? You'll do that for me?"

"Sure. Why not?"

"OK, well, what do we do?"

"It's like this," Randy said, reading out the information.

"Competitors send in their recipes and The Blue House chefs choose the ten best for the finals. The ten best go to The Blue House to make their recipes. Then the winner gets a job at The Blue House."

"A recipe! Oh, my . . ." said Janine.

"That's OK, isn't it? I'm sure you have lots of recipes."

"I don't know. It needs to be something really, really good, right? I don't cook anything like that."

"What about that chicken you did? That was special."

"No, I can't do chicken." *Anybody can cook chicken,* Janine thought.

"Do it, Janine."

"Really?"

"Yes, really. It was great."

"Well . . ." Janine started writing the recipe.

"It needs a name," she said. "I don't have a name for it."

They both thought for a moment.

"I got it!" Randy said. "Chicken Janine!"

"Chicken Janine. Are you crazy?" They were both laughing.

"Do you have a better name?" Randy asked.

Janine wrote it down. "Maybe I really am crazy."

"Chicken Janine!" a woman's voice said. "Interesting . . ."

Janine looked up to see a tall, slim, pretty young woman with long, dark red hair. She wore expensive clothes, Janine saw.

"Oh . . . hi, Hilary," said Randy.

Hilary smiled a big smile at Randy. She turned to Janine. "I'm Hilary," she said, with her big smile. *That doesn't look like a real smile to me,* Janine thought.

"I'm Janine," said Janine.

"Oh," Hilary replied. "I see."

Maybe Chicken Janine wasn't a great idea, Janine thought.

"Hey, Janine, this is my friend I told you about. Hilary's in the cooking competition too."

"You work in the kitchens here, don't you?" Hilary said to Janine.

"That's right," said Janine, smiling back at her.

"Listen, Janine, we need to finish this soon," Randy said.

"I have to go, too," Hilary said. "Bye, Randolph. Nice to meet you, Janine."

Hilary left.

"Randolph?" Janine asked.

"Well, that's my name," he says. "But only Hilary and my mother call me Randolph."

"You two are very close, then . . ." Janine said.

"Well, we were. I mean, she was my girlfriend. But now we're just friends."

"Just friends," said Janine. She felt herself getting angry. *What's wrong with me?* she asked herself.

"Are you all right?" Randy asked.

"Of course I'm all right!" she said. *Janine, slow down,* she told herself.

"Sorry, Randy. I'm just tired. Let's finish this."

◇◇◇

Randy drove to Seattle with Janine's entry form later that day. Then they waited. Days went by, then a week. Janine worked a lot of extra hours to get the money for her rent, and some days Randy looked after Amber so she could work.

Two weeks went by, but Janine didn't hear from The Blue House. Now it was Saturday, the day before the competition. She arrived home after work. Randy and Amber were playing in the living room. The babysitter was there, too.

"Hey," Randy said.

"Mommy, Randy's teaching me to play football!" Amber said.

"That's great. I think." Janine sat down. After working a fifty-hour week, she was very tired. Fifty hours of Gayle King shouting at her.

"Any mail?" Janine asked.

"Just this," Randy said. It was a letter, asking her for rent money. "Listen, Janine? I saw Hilary yesterday. She told me, um . . ."

"She's in the finals?" Janine said. "Of the competition?"

"They called her on Wednesday."

"Well, that's great," Janine said.

"You know," Randy began, "I was thinking. I know you don't have a lot of money at the moment. I can help you out, you know, if you . . ."

Suddenly, the phone rang. Janine looked at it.

"It's a Seattle number," she said.

"Answer it!" Randy told her.

"Hello?"

"Hello, is this Mrs. Janine Cole?"

"Speaking."

"This is Marie Ducasse at The Blue House. I'm sorry we didn't call you earlier. I am happy to tell you that you are in the finals of the cooking competition. Please come tomorrow at one o'clock to The Blue House."

Chapter 4

The Blue House

The Blue House restaurant was full of people. The TV news were there, the newspapers were there, too. The head chef at The Blue House, Georges Ducasse, was one of the six judges who would decide the best recipe. Ducasse was one of the best chefs in the country and had three Michelin stars. The other judges were famous chefs in the city, and there was a food writer from the *Seattle Daily News*. The rest of the people were friends and family of the contestants. Amber was with the babysitter, so only Randy sat in the restaurant. He smiled at her.

Janine went into the big restaurant kitchen. The other competitors were there, waiting to start work at one o'clock. Janine quickly took off her jacket and took out her chicken, vegetables, and other food. When she was ready, she looked around at the others. There were four other women and five men. One of them was Hilary Johnson, Randy's "friend." There were ten tables for them to work at. Of course Hilary was at the next table. Janine felt her face go red.

"Are you all ready with the chicken, Janine?" Hilary asked. Janine didn't like the way she said her name.

"Yes, thanks," said Janine. "What are you making?"

"Oh, I'm doing a new style of *filet du boeuf.*"

"Sounds great," said Janine.

Filet, she thought. *That's about the most expensive meat you can buy.*

What's everyone else making? she asked herself. She looked around, and she saw all the other cooks had expensive meat and fish, and lots of interesting foods. Nobody else had chicken.

"Begin!" said Chef Ducasse, and all the cooks started to make their recipes. They had just an hour and a half to get everything ready and cooked. Janine started to cut the onions and other vegetables. Then she cut the chicken and started to cook it with the onions. She put in the lemon last. Janine worked quickly and well. Soon she was ready to put the chicken and other things into the oven to cook.

Janine looked down at her food. It looked so simple. *So cheap,* she thought. She looked at all the other competitors, making expensive, beautiful food. Her head dropped. *What are you doing here?* she asked herself. *Do you really think you can win? It's just a stupid dream, Janine. Your place is at work, so you can pay the rent! That's your life, Janine, making burgers and fries. Not this.*

Janine suddenly felt hot. She wanted to cry. She looked out at the restaurant. Randy was there, watching her.

He looked worried and got up and came toward the kitchen. Janine went out to talk to him.

"Janine, what is it?" he asked. "What's wrong?"

"Everything," Janine said.

"I don't understand."

"Look at what everyone else is making, and I've got some cheap chicken. It's stupid. I need to be at work, making money. This is just some silly dream. Oh, what am I doing here?"

"Janine, what're you talking about? Your food's great. It doesn't matter how expensive it is. It's about your cooking. It's not about money."

"That's easy for you to say," said Janine. "You've got a rich family. You've always had money. You say it's not about money? Everything is about money. When you don't have money, you understand that."

"Janine, I told you. Don't worry about money. I can help you."

"Help me?" she asked. "You just want to help me? I understand now. Helping with Amber, helping with money . . . You feel sorry for me, don't you? The single mother, with no husband. Helping me makes you feel good, does it?"

"Janine, stop it. You know it's not like that."

Janine was shouting now, but she didn't care. "Say it. Say you're helping me because you feel sorry for me. Say it!"

"Janine, I'm not helping you because I feel sorry for you. I'm helping you because I love you!"

Janine stopped. She felt herself go very red.

"Hey." Randy put his hands on her arms and his face came close to hers. "I love you, Janine," he said. "I love you and I believe in you. Now can you please go back into the kitchen and finish cooking?"

Oh, Janine, she thought. *You really are stupid . . .*

She looked up at him.

"Kiss me first," she said.

So he did.

◇◇◇

"Ladies and gentlemen," Chef Ducasse said. "The food made by each one of our ten cooks today was very, very good. It was hard for the judges to decide. Everyone showed they knew how to cook. So, how to choose the best one? Well, we felt that one dish was very special. It was special because it wasn't expensive or difficult to make . . ."

No . . ., Janine thought.

". . . but it was cooked beautifully. It was like the food my mother gave to me when I was a little boy in France—simple and beautiful, and made with love."

"It's you," Randy said.

No!

"It was, as we French say, *superbe*," Chef Ducasse went on. "The winner is someone who I will be very happy to have in the kitchen of The Blue House as a trainee chef. Ms. Janine Cole, welcome to The Blue House!"

Chapter 5

A new kitchen

Janine heard her name, but she couldn't believe it. People were clapping their hands and saying "Good job!"

Then Georges Ducasse walked up to Janine and kissed her on both cheeks in the French way. "Very good, young lady," he said. All the judges came to her and said, "Good job!"

"Welcome to The Blue House," Chef Ducasse went on. "I hope you can start soon."

"Well . . . I . . . yes . . ." It was all a big surprise to Janine, and she didn't know what to say. Still, she thought, this was what she wanted, wasn't it? She could leave her job in the college cafeteria and move to Seattle with Amber. It wasn't far after all. And what about Randy? Well, Randy could visit her if he wanted to . . .

"Um, excuse me, Monsieur Ducasse." Hilary came forward and spoke to Chef Ducasse. She was holding a piece of paper in her hand.

"Oui?"

"Isn't this competition for *amateur* cooks?" asked Hilary.

The room went quiet.

"Why, yes, but . . ." said Ducasse.

"And doesn't 'amateur' mean 'not working as a cook'—not a professional?" Hilary was reading from the paper now. It was a list of rules of the competition.

"Well . . . yes."

"Well if those are the rules of this competition," said Hilary, "then Janine Cole can't win it. In fact she can't even be a competitor."

"And why is that?" asked Chef Ducasse.

"Because she's a working cook," said Hilary. "She works in a college cafeteria." Hilary looked very happy with herself.

Chef Ducasse looked at Janine. "Is this true?" he asked.

Janine didn't know what to say.

"A college cafeteria?" the chef went on. "Like fries and burgers, you mean?"

"Yes," said Janine, quietly.

Ducasse turned to his wife, Marie.

"Is that really cooking?" Marie asked.

"Well," the chef said. "I'm not sure."

Suddenly, Janine had an idea.

"Could you all wait a moment, please?"

Everyone watched as she took out her phone and called a number.

"Yes?" Gayle King answered.

"It's Janine Cole here," Janine said.

"What do you want, Janine?" Gayle asked.

"Nothing. I just phoned to tell you I want to quit. I'm leaving the cafeteria, Gayle." She put down the phone.

"I'm an amateur now," she said to Chef Ducasse. He smiled.

"Very good. So once again, welcome to The Blue House, Ms. Cole."

"But, it says here . . ." Hilary began.

Ducasse took the paper from her hand.

"This is my restaurant, young miss. And, by the way, your *filet du boeuf* had too much salt. Far too much!"

Hilary's face went red. She walked quickly out of the restaurant.

◇◇◇

Two weeks later, Randy, Janine, and Amber were in Janine's new apartment in Seattle. There were boxes everywhere. Randy and Amber sat on the sofa. Janine was walking around the room. In an hour she would start at The Blue House, and she was nervous.

"Janine, sit down," Randy said.

"Sit down, Mommy," said Amber.

"Good girl!" Randy said to Amber.

Janine smiled and sat down.

"Maybe the babysitter won't come," Janine said.

Then there was a noise at the door.

"She's here!" said Janine, jumping up.

"Janine, relax," said Randy, opening the door. The babysitter was a friend of Randy's younger sister, a girl called Laney.

"Hi, everyone," said Laney. "I'm not late, am I?"

"You're right on time," said Randy.

"Now, if there's a problem, please call," said Janine to Laney.

"Everything will be fine," said Randy. "Let's go now. Bye, Amber."

"Bye, Randy," said the little girl.

"Say bye to Mommy," Janine said. She kissed her little girl and held her.

"Bye, Mommy. Don't put too much salt in," Amber said.

"I won't," Janine said with a smile.

Ten minutes later, Randy and Janine arrived at The Blue House in Randy's car. They got out and stood outside the restaurant.

"Well, here we are," he said. "Are you feeling OK?"

"I guess so. I'm nervous. It's like a dream, Randy. I can't believe it."

"Me neither," he said, looking at her. Then he kissed her.

"Oh, Randy," she said. "I don't know what to say. Thank you. So much. For everything. You know, I never thought . . ."

"Shh, Janine. You don't need to say anything. Anyway, I think we both did very well. Now get in there, girl. Show them what you can do."

"OK," Janine said. She opened the car door. "Do you really think it'll be OK? Maybe they won't like my other food . . ."

Randy smiled.

"Go on, Janine," he said. "You know you can do it."

They both laughed.

"OK, then," she said.

Janine opened the door to the restaurant and walked inside.

Review

A. Match the characters in the story to their descriptions.

1. _____ Janine Cole

2. _____ Amber Cole

3. _____ Randy Gordon

4. _____ Hilary Johnson

5. _____ Gayle King

6. _____ Georges Ducasse

a. Randy's ex-girlfriend

b. head chef at The Blue House

c. Janine's three-year-old daughter

d. a mother who works in the college cafeteria

e. a student at Brenton College and a football player

f. manager of the college cafeteria

B. Read each statement and circle whether it is true (T) or false (F).

1. Janine went to the bank to put in some money.   T / F

2. Amber thinks her mother uses too much salt in her food.   T / F

3. Janine's husband died in a car crash.   T / F

4. "Randy" is short for "Randall."   T / F

5. Randy still has feelings for Hilary.   T / F

6. The Blue House competition is a small event.   T / F

7. Janine is the only one in the competition who cooks chicken.   T / F

8. Randy is helping Janine because he feels sorry for her.   T / F

C. Choose the best answer for each question.

1. What did Janine used to do before her husband died?
   a. She was studying communications at Brenton.
   b. She was studying to be a chef.
   c. She was working in a restaurant.
   d. She was already working at the cafeteria.

2. How does Randy know about the cooking competition?
   a. Janine told him about it.
   b. Hilary told him about it.
   c. He read about it in the newspapers.
   d. He knows the person who runs the restaurant.

3. According to Randy, who calls him by his full name?
   a. only Hilary
   b. Hilary and his mother
   c. all his friends
   d. his whole family

4. Why does Chef Ducasse think Janine's dish is special?
   a. The dish has very expensive ingredients.
   b. Janine spent a lot of time and effort cooking it.
   c. She had used an old French recipe.
   d. The dish was simple, yet done very well.

5. Hilary says Janine shouldn't win the competition because _____.
   a. she works in the school cafeteria
   b. she got a lot of help from Randy
   c. she used to go to cooking school
   d. her cooking is not good enough

D. Write the name of the character who said the words.

1. "Well, if those are the rules of the competition, then Janine Cole can't win it. In fact, she can't even be a competitor." _____

2. "You can't just shout at customers that way. I'm afraid you can't work here anymore. Please get your things and go . . ." _____

3. "Your food's great. It doesn't matter how expensive it is. It's about your cooking. It's not about money." _____

4. "It's stupid. I need to be at work, making money. This is just some silly dream. Oh, what am I doing here?" _____

5. "This is my restaurant, young miss. And, by the way, your *filet du boeuf* had too much salt. Far too much!" _____

Janine Cole

Georges Ducasse

Randy Gordon

Hilary Johnson

Gayle King

E. Complete each sentence with the correct word from the box.

amateur	chef	babysitter	judge
recipe	rules	trainee	form

1. A(n) _____ is a set of instructions used to cook food.

2. A(n) _____ does something for fun and not as a job.

3. A(n) _____ decides who wins a competition.

4. A(n) _____ is someone who cooks at a restaurant.

5. A(n) _____ takes care of children for money.

6. A(n) _____ learns on the job and does not have much experience.

7. _____ are instructions telling what you can or cannot do.

8. You fill out a(n) _____ with your information.

Background Reading:
Spotlight on ... *MasterChef*

MasterChef (US) is a cooking competition shown on American television. The show was started by a famous chef called Gordon Ramsay.

Amateur cooks from all over the United States signed up to be contestants on the show. They were not professional chefs, just people who loved to cook. This show gave them a chance to prove how good they were at it.

Each week they had to cook different types of food. Then, their food was judged by Ramsay and two other judges. Sometimes they were given challenges, such as cooking for a birthday party, or running a restaurant for a night. They also had to use recipes based on a theme chosen by the judges. In episode three, the theme was to use a single egg!

The winner of the first MasterChef was Whitney Miller, a 22-year-old college student from Mississippi. She won $250,000 and the chance to write a cookbook. Ramsay said Miller was an amateur cook at the beginning of the show, but now she cooks like a professional.

Gordon Ramsay was born in Scotland, but grew up in England. He wanted to be a professional soccer player when he was younger, until an injury forced him to look for a different job. He then trained as a chef at various restaurants in London and Paris.

Ramsay opened his first restaurant in 1998 when he was 31 years old. Since then, he has been awarded a total of 12 Michelin stars for the quality of his food. In 2001, he became one of only three chefs in the United Kingdom to hold three Michelin stars at one time.

Ramsay now owns restaurants all over the world. He has written many cookbooks and even has his own television shows in the United Kingdom, Australia, and the United States.

Think About It

1. Do you enjoy cooking? Have you ever cooked a meal for someone?

2. Do you need to take classes to become a good cook? Or do you think you can learn on your own?

Spotlight on ... *Michelin Stars*

What is the Michelin Guide?

The Michelin Guide is a series of restaurant guide books for major cities around the world. They award "stars" to restaurants based on the quality of their food and their surroundings. Winning Michelin stars is the life goal of many professional chefs, and is not easy to achieve.

Who awards these stars?

Restaurants are visited by anonymous judges, meaning the restaurants don't know these people are from the Michelin Guide. The judges are professionals with a background in the restaurant business. They usually visit the restaurant a few times, and they always pay their own bills.

What do the star ratings mean?

* One star: A very good restaurant in its category.
* Two stars: Excellent cooking. First-class cuisine of its type.
* Three stars: Exceptional cuisine and worth a special journey. Often extremely expensive, and with a big wine list.

Winning a single Michelin star is a huge achievement for a restaurant, and getting two or three stars is very rare. The 2009 Michelin Guide to France lists 3,531 restaurants, but just 548 received stars. 449 of these restaurants received one star, 73 received two stars, and only 26 received three. As of late 2009, there are only 81 three-star restaurants in the world.

Think About It

1. What is the best restaurant you have ever been to? What was the food like?

2. Some people travel all over the world to eat at different restaurants. How far would you travel for food, and why?

Spotlight on . . . *Fun Food Facts*

Do you know...

- The average person eats 680 kg of food each year, including 68 kg of meat, 132 kg of milk and cream, 16 kg of eggs, 22 kg of chicken, 31 kg of bread, 57 kg of potatoes, 37 kg of fruit, and 23 kg of chocolate!

- 25% of an apple is air.

- The tomato is actually a fruit.

- Apples are more effective than coffee in waking you up in the morning.

- Peanuts are used to make dynamite.

- The original Coca-Cola drink was green.

- Honey is the only food which does not go bad.

- Most French fries sold in fast food restaurants are coated in sugar so they will turn brown.

- The world's hottest pepper (Bhut jolokia from India) is so hot you need gloves to touch it.

- The largest food ever cooked was a roast camel in Saudi Arabia.

- People first made instant coffee in the 18th century.

- There's a higher chance you'll be hungry if you are cold than if you are hot.

Think About It

1. Which of the above is the most surprising?

2. Do you know any other fun food facts?

Glossary

amateur	(*n.*)	someone who is not a professional
cafeteria	(*n.*)	a cheap student restaurant at a college
chef	(*n.*)	someone who cooks in a restaurant
babysitter	(*n.*)	someone who takes care of children for money
cook	(*v.*)	to make food
competition	(*n.*)	an event where people try to win a prize
form	(*n.*)	a paper people write on when they give information to a company
fries	(*n.*)	fried potatoes
judge	(*n.*)	someone who decides who will win a competition
manager	(*n.*)	the boss
Michelin star	(*n.*)	a system that decides the best restaurants in the world
nervous	(*adj.*)	a little worried, e.g., before a test
quit	(*v.*)	If you quit your job, you stop working there and look for work elsewhere.
recipe	(*n.*)	a set of instructions to cook food such as Chicken Janine or spaghetti
rent	(*n.*)	the money you need to pay for an apartment every month
rules	(*n.*)	instructions to tell you what you can and cannot do
salt	(*n.*)	a white seasoning used in cooking to add taste
special	(*adj.*)	unusual
taste	(*n.*)	Your sense of taste allows you to identify which food you have in your mouth.
trainee	(*n.*)	a student learning something on the job, e.g., a trainee chef, a trainee manager